Bigleaf Sugaring
Tapping the western maple

Gary Backlund
Katherine Backlund

Backwoods Forest Management, Ladysmith, BC 2012

Copyright © 2004 Gary Backlund and Katherine Backlund
Second Edition 2012

All rights reserved. The use of any part of this publication reproduced, transmitted in any form or by any means, electronic, mechanical, photocopying, recording, or otherwise, or stored in a retrieval system, without the proper consent of the publisher, is an infringement of the copyright law.

Nation Library of Canada Cataloguing in Publication Data

Backlund, Gary, 1951-
Bigleaf Sugaring: Tapping the western maple
Gary Backlund, Katherine Backlund

Includes index
ISBN 0-9736206-0-9

1. Tree tapping—Northwest, Pacific.
2. Maple Syrup.
3. Acer macrophyllum.
I. Backlund, Katherine, 1986- II. Title.

TP395.B32 2004   633.6'4   C2004-904665-9

Published by
Backwoods Forest Management
12691 South Doole Road
Ladysmith, British Columbia   V9G 1J6

Edited by Teesh Backlund
Cover design by Gary, Teesh and Katherine Backlund
Photos by Gary and Katherine Backlund, unless noted

Printed and bound in Canada

Contents

Acknowledgements 7
Forward 10
Introduction 13
   By Katherine 13
   By Gary 15
About bigleaf maple tapping 18
Getting started 23
   Tapping season 23
   Before the season starts 23
   Scale of operation 24
   Equipment and supplies 25
Sap flow and tree dynamics 27
   Sap flow 27
   Tree dynamics 29
Tapping the trees 34
   Identifying bigleaf maple 34
   Choosing the trees 35
   Drilling 39
Sap collection and handling 42
   Spiles 42
   Plumbing 43
   Containers 45
   Collection and storage 47
   Filtering 49

Evaporation and syrup making 51
Evaporators 51
Boiling down 55
Finishing 57
Bottling and storage 62
Syrup grading rules 63
Flavour wheel for maple products 66

Ending the season 69
When to call it quits 69
Pulling the taps 69
Cleaning the equipment 70

Tree stand management 73
Habitat 73
Tree health 74
Spacing the stand 75
Coppice control 76
Harvesting for lumber 77

Appendix A—Recipes 81
Maple sap 81
Maple syrup 83

Appendix B—Equipment Sources 86
Equipment suppliers 86
Other sources of information 87

Appendix C—Glossary of Terms 88

Index 92

Three good producing trees will yield enough sap to produce four litres of syrup per year

The crew at Backwoods
Katherine, Teesh and Gary (left to right)

Bigleaf Sugaring

Acknowledgements

First and foremost, we thank Harold Macy and the BC Small Woodland and Master Woodland Manager programs for introducing us to maple sugaring and other non-timber forest products. We also thank the British Columbia Agroforestry Fund for their interest and support of our efforts to create a commercial West Coast maple sugaring industry.

There's been a lot to learn through successes and failures. Fellow sapsuckers, Lawrence Lampson, Louis Lapi, Bram Lucieer, Harold Macy and Jay Rastogi, have freely shared what they have learned about bigleaf sugaring. They continue to be an inspiration every time we start to feel that sugaring is becoming too much like work.

Harold has spent more than twenty years promoting bigleaf maple sugaring. Through his efforts, the potential for a commercial bigleaf maple sugaring industry has caught the attention of British Columbia's Agroforestry program. Harold was instrumental in getting Vancouver Island's first commercial evaporator set up at what was the University of British Columbia's (UBC) research farm at Oyster River near Campbell River. Although not part of the UBC program, this evaporator allowed us to take a couple of giant steps up the learning curve in regard to maple sugaring. We are also thankful for the support from a few transplanted easterners that taught us how to run an evaporator and make syrup on a larger scale.

Bram contributed many hours setting up the UBC sugar shack and evaporator, and helped most of us with operating this equipment. There were quite a few twelve-hour shifts running the evaporator. Bram was part of most of these long days, filtering sap, stoking the fire and skimming the foam. Bram's been a co-presenter for many of the workshops and talks we've given. He also makes incredible maple sap wine, which we all continue to enjoy. Lastly, Bram pioneered the tapping of coppices, a real boost to production for many of us.

Lawrence and Louis have both boosted our morale and given us tours of their maple sugaring projects. Each have sites that are somewhat different geoclimatically than ours. They are successfully tapping trees that we wouldn't have tried. We've learned a lot from both of them. Lawrence is the one that taught the group how to clarify syrup with egg. Both Lawrence and Louis have taken syrup making to a level approaching an art, producing in-

Making syrup at Oyster River

credibly great tasting syrup.

Jay is the manager of Merv Wilkinson's Wildwood forest and a leader in the field of ecoforestry. For the first few years, Jay and Kiwi Cove Lodge organized a two-day maple sugaring workshop that was both educational and entertaining, plus the workshops contain three wonderful meals and great snacks where every dish had maple sap or syrup as an ingredient. After eating and drinking so much maple-enhanced foods most of us leave this event feeling we could grow big and strong like a maple tree. We always enjoy our visits with Jay as his outlook on life and love of nature is contagious. We feel good after spending time with him, plus it's always a learning opportunity.

As always, special thanks go to Katherine's mom / Gary's wife, Teesh Backlund, for her editing, proofing and encouragement. This is the fifth book that she has cheerfully helped with. Like the other Vancouver Island sugaring wives, not only has her kitchen been invaded over and over, but she has put in hours collecting sap, feeding fires, filtering and finishing syrup.

Lastly, thank you to the BC Forest Discovery Centre in Duncan. For the past five years they have hosted our annual *Bigleaf Maple Syrup Festival* on the first Saturday of February. They have also hosted the festival debriefing meeting, which is a well attended maple recipe potluck extravaganza.

Gary Backlund
Katherine Backlund

Forward

As my bit cut into the first stem I saw how wet the sawdust was—I knew I had a gusher. The barometer had been swinging back and forth over the last few days. Normally I want a few good days in a row of high pressure and then a change to a low-pressure system. This almost always gives a good sap flow. It was the morning of December 27th and around 10 A.M. Tearing myself away from some technical writing that had been chaining me to a computer for most of the month, I headed outdoors. The ground was damp and the tops of the cars had a dusting of corn snow. The temperature was hovering near the freezing mark.

Grabbing sidecutters, a hammer, a brace & bit, a handful of spiles and tees, some tubing and two 16-litre plastic buckets, I walked about 200 metres to one of our patches of Vancouver

Drilling the old fashioned way

Bigleaf Sugaring

Island sugarbush. About ten years ago we had taken down a very large maple there. The following year we had about 30 coppices (shoots) growing from that stump. Once they were about three years old, I reduced the number to five. When my back was turned, the stump produced about seven more. These were now between 10 and 25 cm in diameter (4 – 10 in).

Today I was going to tap these twelve coppice stems. I had started the day by putting on longjohns. Before going outdoors I donned a Stanfield top, my work coat and a touque. There was a clear deep blue sky with only a few clouds on the horizon. Patches of hoar frost stood where the sun hadn't touched the ground.

As I pulled the bit out of the first stem the sap did more than just drip. I had a spile ready with a 60 cm (24 in) long tube attached to it. The spile was quickly pounded in. Holding the tube in the air as high as I could, I pulled the bucket into place. The sap actually ran uphill in the tube to the top and overflowed within 15 or 20 seconds. There was a lot of pressure in that tree!

I inserted the tube into the bucket and drilled the next hole. The tube from that spile got spliced into the first tube using a tee. Soon I had four more spiles connected and I installed a vented seventh spile at the end of the run. The sap flow was incredible and my bucket already had a couple inches of sap. Needless to say, my hands and tools were getting sticky.

The other five stems were tapped and plumbed into the second bucket. In the short time I took to tap these additional five stems, the sap level had risen in the first bucket another two inches. It was noon and surprisingly warm although as I headed to the house for lunch, the ground was still frozen where shaded.

By two o'clock the blue sky had disappeared and the temperature was dropping once again. This coppiced

Forward

stump had now yielded eight litres of sap, but the flow was slowing. Over the next 36 hours, it would produce a total of more than 40 litres. I had five other similar coppiced stumps tapped and several individual trees that were also producing, plus some duds. None were producing as well as this new tapping. Time to fire up our $20 home-built evaporator and make some maple syrup.

Two litres of sap in less than 15 minutes

Introduction

By Katherine

Ever since I can remember, my family has been big into the outdoors. I've grown up on a Managed Forest and have been travelling the trails since before I could walk. Countless hours have been spent exploring this paradise; climbing trees and huge moss covered boulders. One of my earliest memories is sitting in a cardboard box partially filled with newspaper, deep in the bush while my parents built fire breaks.

My parents were quick to teach me about forestry work, and by age three I was helping plant trees. Brushing, pruning, setting choke and mill cleanup soon followed. These tasks were enjoyable, and seemed more like play than work.

Growing up in a managed forest
(photo by Jim Lettic)

As I got older I began practicing forestry on my own, and by my mid-teens was harvesting cedar and sequoia greens for the Christmas floral market. I also started growing maple seedlings for sale in my small tree nursery.

Since my dad became interested in tapping maple trees, I have been involved in all aspects of our maple sugaring project and really enjoy this non-timber forest activity. If you decide to make homemade maple syrup, the benefits are enormous. They include an excuse to get outside and take pleasure from the fresh winter air, a great smelling house and a wonderful tasty treat to top your ice cream.

On a side note, Jay and Nina Rastogi introduced us to eating young bigleaf maple flowers. The flowers can be steamed and eaten like broccoli, however the Rastogi's favourite is maple flower quiche.

By Gary

I was skeptical when Harold Macy, our instructor, spoke about tapping western maple trees. Learning to be a Master Woodland Manager, I was midway through four months of training at the Mesachie Lake Forest Research Station near Lake Cowichan. I thought I knew quite a bit about local forestry until I began taking this training.

My wife, Teesh and daughter, Katherine and I own British Columbia's Managed Forest #127. It's not large as far as forests go, just a little over 29 hectares (72 acres) located on a south sloping hillside overlooking Ladysmith Harbour. You'd call it a woodlot anywhere else outside of BC, but here that name's already used for small government forest licenses. This confuses a lot of people, but *Managed Forest* sounds more impressive than *woodlot,* so we're happy. As far as the management that the name implies, the trees do most of the work, we just help things along a bit. It's sort of like trying to herd wild deer, you can have a lot of effect, but you have little control.

When we bought our property twenty-four years ago it had a large component of Vancouver Island's very prolific maple species, the bigleaf maple. We were somewhat newcomers to forestry at the time and the Registered Professional Foresters that we consulted suggested that we might try to do some stand conversion away from maple and towards growing more conifers. They must have said this a bit tongue-in-cheek as it's not easy to do. Bigleaf maples are resilent—cut them down and they'll grow up to 60 more coppice stems from the stump. Even if you burn the stump they'll come back. And seeds! Those little helicopters fly everywhere.

Not heeding the foresters' advice, we decided that if our forest liked growing maples then we would try to develop markets for this under-utilized tree. Sure enough

Introduction

we did, and in the end we found that we can make more money with this species than any other we grow.

So back to my being skeptical. Harold had this old canning jar containing a dark honey coloured liquid that he said was bigleaf maple syrup. He passed out some spoons and then passed the jar around the room. I guess I had visions of it tasting like turpentine, but when my turn came, I was suitably impressed. It tasted like maple syrup—only better!

I was instantly converted. I bought some spiles—that's the name of those little pipes that get stuck into the trees—and after class drove home and tapped three trees. Beginner's luck shone on me, the weather conditions were just right and before the drill bit came out of the tree the sap was flowing! Within 36 hours I had 40 litres of maple sap—all from only three of my several thousand maple trees. My evaporation equipment was pretty basic back then. I was kept busy processing sap almost daily until the season ended a month or so later.

Now when I speak to people about tapping maples, I try to give credit where credit's due and tell them Harold made a sapsucker out of me. Although we already enjoyed the benefits of a healthy diet, since we learned about maple sugaring, our menus have been enhanced by the addition of numerous gourmet dishes produced with maple sap and syrup. The sap goes into many recipes in lieu of water and we use the syrup in all kinds of cooking.

This book is meant to pass on what I've learned from my successes and failures and from people like Harold, Bram and other western sapsuckers. Our climate and tree species are quite different from back east, and this creates some interesting challenges and opportunities. If you decide to give sapsucking a try, I hope you find this book useful. Good luck and may your sugar run at 3%.

About bigleaf maple tapping

Tapping maple trees for sap and syrup is easy and requires little in the way of equipment and tools. Making syrup isn't that difficult either. However, like wine there is a knack to making really fine syrup. The tapping for sap and boiling to produce syrup is known as *sugaring*.

Sugaring is quite enjoyable, plus it adds to a healthy lifestyle in many ways. It's another reason to smile and look forward to the grey days of winter. All too often during that season, many of us find it hard to get outside for a little exercise. However, once we do get out, we're usually happy that we made the effort. So even if the sap isn't flowing, maple tapping is making us healthier. And if the sap is flowing, we end up with nutritional benefits from adding maple sap and syrup to our diet.

If it's big and a maple, and it's located in the Pacific Northwest, then the chances are you've found a bigleaf maple. Also known as western maple, Oregon maple and broadleaf maple; bigleaf maple is North America's second most abundant species of hardwood. In British Columbia it ranges south from Bella Bella and west from the Coast Mountains. Large stands range over most of Vancouver Island from Alert Bay all the way down to Victoria. In the US it can be found west of the Cascade Mountains from Washington all the way down to southern California.

So is this tree species a good one to tap for making maple syrup? According to several tree and plant books, the answer is yes. However, many people believed that it had to compete with eastern syrup to be commercially viable. People judged the sap as not being sweet enough. Some thought the syrup flavour substandard because the taste was stronger than the pancake syrup they were used to. The tapping season was also thought to be very much shorter than it really is. So here's some information to help change these misconceptions.

- Sweetness of bigleaf maple sap runs about 2% sugar. This is about 1% lower than the average for eastern sugar maple. It takes about 40 to 50 litres of bigleaf sap to make one litre of syrup.
- In blind taste tests, bigleaf maple syrup flavour often wins over eastern maple syrup, but it's much stronger than its eastern cousin. For some it may not be ideal for waffles and French toast, but that extra flavour excels when used in cooking meats, fish, vegetables, and baked beans or for use in desserts. Try some on fruit and/or vanilla ice cream and you'll be amazed!
- Tapping can start as early as November and the season sometimes continues into early March. Sap harvests can reach 200 litres per tree using only a single spile.

The process

So how does one go about sugaring? Sap is mostly water. It's collected by drilling a short hole into the tree and "tapping" a tapered pipe (called a spile) into the opening. Due to the tree's interior pressure, sap is pushed into this hole and out the spile to a collection bucket. Buckets are emptied every few days and the sap is boiled to evaporate off water until the sugar level reaches 66.5%.

At that point it's considered maple syrup. This process requires no additives or preservatives, but filtering at two or three stages during the process is beneficial.

East and west sugaring differences

Our bigleaf maple tree species and Pacific Northwest climate is very different from back east. There the trees and sap are frozen solid most of the winter, which stops the sap flow. They have a two to four week tapping season, whereas the west can have a three month season if the weather cooperates.

In the east the larger diameter trees are tapped, but out west we have better results tapping smaller diameter trees. Due to the lower sugar content of the western maples, more sap is required to produce the same amount of syrup. This extra amount of sap translates into higher energy costs, but also gives more flavour to the syrup.

Unlike the sugar maple, bigleaf maples are very resilent and, in fact, are almost impossible to kill when they are growing where not wanted. Because of this, in the past, much of the management information available for bigleaf maple was how to slow or prevent it from growing.

Bigleaf maple is native to British Columbia, Washington, Oregon, and California

Abundance, range, and use

It is estimated that there are over two hundred million cubic metres of bigleaf maple in the Pacific Northwest. Despite its abundance it is very underutilized. Common uses for bigleaf maple include firewood, chips for smoking meat and fish, woodturning and other artisan uses, veneer and a small amount of milling for lumber. Milling bigleaf maple for lumber is currently growing at a fast pace and it will most likely experience the same phenomenal growth that happened to the red alder lumber market.

Tapping bigleaf maple is not a new concept; individuals have done it at a hobby level for at least forty years. Due to lower sugar content than some of the eastern maples, tapping our western maple was thought to be not economically viable. This is probably true when thinking "inside the box" of the market for bulk wholesale breakfast syrup. Due to changes in socioeconomic conditions over the last ten years, commercial tapping of bigleaf maple now looks quite viable.

Although syrup is the traditional use, maple sap also has many uses. It can be substituted for water in most recipes, such as when cooking rice, making soup, baking bread, and for making hot beverages such as coffee and tea. Rice cooked with maple water (sap) has a slight sweetness and hint of maple flavour. Bread tends to have a better rise when using maple water. The most important benefit of maple water is its nutritional value.

Maple water contains minerals including calcium, potassium, manganese, magnesium, phosphorus and iron. It contains vitamins B2, B5, B6, niacin, biotin, malic acid, folic acid and trace amounts of amino acids. Markets through natural food stores can be developed and maple water for cooking can also be promoted to restaurants. Both maple water (sap) and syrup can be marketed as being organic.

Maple wine made from maple water is currently being produced on Vancouver Island on a large-scale hobby basis with the intent of creating a commercial industry. There is a huge tourism potential for this product. Currently much of the wine being made is of commercial quality and has been very well received by the many people who have sampled it.

Getting started

Tapping season

The tapping season is very site and weather dependent. In general it runs from when the leaves come off the trees until the new spring buds are ready to burst open. Tree buds will use large amounts of the tree's sugar, plus their late stage development degrades the flavour of the sap, giving it a taste that is referred to as *buddy*.

In general, the tapping season is from November until some time in early March. The best flows and sweetest sap usually occur in December and January. If your site is either farther inland from the coast, at a higher elevation, towards the southern or northern range for the species, or on a north slope, you may find these dates need to be adjusted. It's also weather dependent in regard to the arrival of fall and spring being either early or late for any given year. The timing of the tapping season is also affected by the height of the water table, number of frosts, snows and cold spells mother nature throws at the trees.

Before the season starts

So what should you do while waiting for the season to start (besides reading this book)? The short list is to
- determine your scale of operation
- acquire your equipment

- determine where you plan to do your boiling down
- pick out the trees to tap while their leaves make them easy to identify, and
- do a bit of brushing and path building if needed

Scale of operation

Determine the scale of operation you want to run. This should be based on how much sap you are willing to collect and haul, plus the amount of syrup you want to produce. The equipment you will need will be very different for a 100-spile operation than for a 4-spile set up.

Your first question regarding scale is whether you are going to tap commercially or just for your own use. Like many, we started small with just a few spiles and could easily handle the sap on the kitchen stove or on the family-room woodstove. Fortunately we have a powerful rangehood and a good whole-house ventilation system. Later we progressed to using a propane burner outside under a small tarp-covered hut (sugar shack). This worked fine for processing up to about 50 litres of sap per day.

Trees will yield up to 16 litres per day (4 US gal) of sap, but most will only average 2 – 4 litres and some will be duds. The sap should be collected and processed at least once every three days. In theory, each productive tree will produce 60 litres (15 US gal) of sap per season. Our own experience is that until you get to know your trees, about 30 percent of your tappings will be duds (sap flows so low they won't be worth collecting).

If we work backwards from the amount of syrup you want to produce, you will need about 40 – 50 litres (10 – 12 US gal) to produce 1 litre (1 US quart) of syrup. With this in mind, and if you don't yet know which trees are productive, we recommend that you tap one tree for each litre of syrup you want to produce. In future years, you will know which trees are your best producers and can expect to make closer to 1.5 litres of syrup per tree tapped.

Equipment and supplies

You will need the following equipment. Some will be available locally, but you may need to order some from a maple syrup supply store. (See Appendix B)
- **11 mm (7/16 in) drill bit and drill**—These can be a brace & bit or cordless drill. It should be a twist type bit, not a speed bit (a.k.a. spade bit) as they can clog the sap vessels).
- **Spiles**—We recommend the plastic type with 7 mm (5/16 in) outlets. If used with tubing, these will help keep the tree holes from drying and will only require re-tapping about every five to six weeks as opposed to about every four weeks if using metal spiles.
- **Hammer**—For driving in spiles and pulling them out
- **Tubing**—It should be somewhat stiff and at least semi-transparent. Although clear tubing is available at most hardware and wine making stores, the tubing from a maple syrup supply store is easier to work with and clean. Also, it won't have as great a tendency to sag.
- **Tubing cutter**—Can be a set of hand pruning shears or sheet metal snips
- **Tees**—For use with tubing if you want to connect more than one spile to a container
- **Sap collection containers**—These should be large enough to hold at least 24 hours worth of sap flow and be easy to pour from. You will make collection easier whenever you can collect sap from several spiles into one container. 16-litre (4 US gal) vegetable oil jugs work well and can be obtained free of charge from many restaurants.
- **Large pot or pan for boiling sap**—Ideally it should

have a large surface area for evaporation
- **Filter paper and/or cloth**—Milk filters will work, but maple filter paper and medium weight unbleached cotton cloth are preferable for syrup
- **Candy thermometer**—With graduations of two degrees Fahrenheit or a digital version
- **Brix sap refractometer**—For measuring sugar content of sap (optional and expensive)

For larger operations you will also need a proper evaporator (can be homemade), a small sugar shack to do your boiling-off in, tanks for sap collection and storage, bottles or cans for packaging syrup, and labels for the packaged product. It will also be wise to purchase a Brix syrup refractometer or a syrup hydrometer.

A small and funky sugar shack

26   *Bigleaf Sugaring*

Sap flow and tree dynamics

Sap flow

Winter weather is not consistent from one year to the next, or from month to month. Locale is also a factor, as the Pacific Northwest has many microclimates and weather patterns. In other words, because weather plays an important part in triggering sap flow, each tapping season will be a bit different.

In our area on southern Vancouver Island, the tapping season starts shortly after the leaves have fallen off the trees and continues until almost bud-burst. In reality sap flows year-round, but the sugar content and taste are only desirable for maple sugaring during the dormant season. Once the buds are ready to burst, they are consuming large amounts of sugar resulting in the sap flavour going "buddy."

Although we consider the trees dormant during the winter, the buds continue to develop. In early November the new buds are so small they can hardly be seen. By early December they have doubled in size and are easily visible. Some photosynthesis is taking place through the thin bark on the younger branches during the dormant season.

We usually tap a few trees in early November and have recorded good flows as early as November 7th. The sugar content is a bit lower than it will be a month later, but we're glad to have the sap for cooking and for making a bit of syrup.

Sap flows in November can be hit or miss with good flows and then nothing for two weeks or more. November weather can be anything from Indian summer conditions to snow and freezing. December, January and February can have daily sap runs or next to nothing for weeks on end. Some winters, we get up to five distinct sap runs and other winters give only one poor run. Between sap runs we can have a two or three week period with little or no flow. The flavour of the syrup produced will change from month to month.

Our location is in a warm spot, modulated by Ladysmith Harbour and a southern exposure. Further inland there is more snow and many frosty nights. In some places freezing stops the sap flow and snow makes it difficult to collect sap.

Unless tapping along a stream or wetland, the water table needs to peak before the trees will produce a good sap run.

Every year is different, sometimes the sap runs when you think it should and other times you have perfect weather conditions for a sap run and you get nothing. Sometimes you get large quantities of flow when you least expect it. Although we've read that bigleaf maple gives the best flow during the morning, our trees don't reflect this. The flow can happen any time day or night and can be up to 16 litres (4 U.S. gal) in 24 hours from a single spile. The flow can start like someone opening a valve and can stop just as abruptly. One set of six coppices we tapped ran in a steady stream and gave 4 litres (1 U.S. gal) in 15 minutes. An hour later the weather cooled and it was barely dripping.

Tree dynamics

The common belief is that you want a cold night followed by a warm day for good sap run. Eastern maples may follow this rule, but our western maples seem to have their larger sap runs triggered by other factors.

Chapter 6 of the *North American Maple Syrup Producers Manual* states, "*The Physiology of sap flow in maple trees is a complex biological process which is not completely understood. While it has been the subject of several investigations, the specific nature of the process remains unclear.*"

This was written about the eastern maples, which are much more predictable in regards to sap flow than their western cousin, the bigleaf maple. Our own experiences indicate that a run occurs within a day or two of a weather change, provided the weather isn't changing daily. It seems to be triggered by a warm spell after a cold snap. It can also be triggered by a low pressure system after a few days of high pressure (in other words, some rain or snow after a few days of blue skies).

The *Producers Manual* also states, "*Several aspects of the process are understood, however, and this knowledge can be helpful to maple producers.*" So let's look at what we know about the dynamics of sap flow. According to the *Bigleaf Maple Managers' Handbook for British Columbia*, sap flow is caused by stem pressure. It notes that stem pressure often exceeds root pressure for bigleaf maple, but that it's just the opposite for birch trees.

According to the *Bigleaf Maple Managers' Handbook*, bigleaf maple stems (trunks) absorb water while freezing, and extrude water while thawing, but only if sucrose (sugar) is present. This leads us to expect a sap flow on a warm day after a frosty night. Since wood is a good insulator, it is more probable to need several freezing cold days/nights and then a warm day to get a good sap flow.

Trees don't have blood or veins, but they do have a circulatory system of sorts. The hair-like roots (and maples have lots of these) suck up large amounts of water and dissolved minerals from the ground. This is mixed with a small amount of sugar and protein to form sap and the mixture is pushed up through the sapwood (outer portion of the stem) to the leaves. Known as transpiration, the distance sap must travel upwards can exceed 30 metres (100 ft). The water and dissolved minerals (sap mixture) infuse the leaves and are converted by photosynthesis to sugar and protein. This food travels down through the cambium layer of the bark (part of the phloem) to feed and grow roots and to become part of the sap mixture.

Photosynthesis is an amazing process. Using energy in the form of sunlight, molecules of carbon dioxide combine with water molecules to form glucose ($C_6H_{12}O_2$) and oxygen.

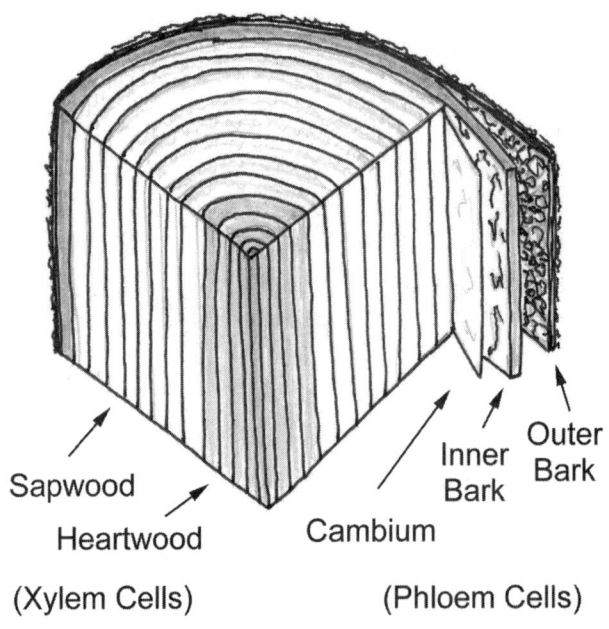

Sapwood
Heartwood
(Xylem Cells)

Cambium
Inner Bark
Outer Bark
(Phloem Cells)

The formula for this process is $6CO_2 + 6H_2O +$ energy $\longrightarrow C_6H_{12}O_2 + 6O_2$. So, not only are leaves like little sugar factories, but they also help reduce greenhouse gas (CO_2) and produce oxygen for the air we breathe.

Maple trees also reverse this process, burning sugar with the released energy and CO_2. This is known as respiration. Fortunately photosynthesis produces about ten

Katherine measuring sugar content of sap using a refractometer

Sap flow and tree dynamics

times more sugar and oxygen than respiration uses.

In trying to understand sap flow, we know that there are two methods for moving sap. One is the cohesiveness of water molecules (tendency to stick together) that pull water up when needed by branches, buds and leaves. The other is by pressure within the stem caused by a buildup of CO_2.

It is believed that temperature change causes the stem to act like a pump in that it sucks water up from the roots, then pressurizes and pushes the sap upwards. This certainly makes sense as we've watched it happen when placing a spile with an attached tube into a tap hole. Holding the tube above the spile, the sap rose straight up in the tube approximately 60 cm (24 in) in about 15 seconds.

In trying to determine what weather conditions will result in the best sap flows, we need to know what triggers a buildup of pressure within the stem, and this is not clearly understood when it comes to bigleaf maple. When stem pressure exceeds atmospheric pressure, sap gets pushed out through tap holes. This is why we sometimes get a sap flow as a low pressure system arrives (rain or snow).

There is also a seasonal phenomenon, when trees suck up more than normal amounts of water. For many trees this is when water (rain) is plentiful. Although for most trees this is in the spring, for bigleaf maple it seems to occur during December and January.

* * *

Although we probably haven't answered all your questions about sap flow and tree dynamics, hopefully our comments on this topic will be helpful to your understanding of sap flow and sugaring. It is wise to invest in a Brix refractometer or sugar hydrometer to measure sugar levels during different parts of the sugaring season.

At times early in the season, we can collect large quantities of sap, but it's running at less than 1% sugar. It will take 100 litres of sap to make one litre of poor quality syrup. While the sap may be good for cooking, it's not worth turning into syrup, and probably we shouldn't be drilling too many extra holes in our trees.

We encourage you to experiment and strongly recommend that you keep records of your successes and failures.

Tapping the trees

Identifying bigleaf maple
(Acer macrophyllum)

The first step in choosing which trees to tap is to make sure you choose maple and not cottonwood or alder trees. It's easiest to identify your trees while the leaves are still on. Bigleaf maple is North America's second most abundant hardwood species. If you live near the West Coast, most large native maples trees you find will be bigleaf. British Columbia, for example, has three native maple tree species, but only the bigleaf grows to tree size.

Most people can identify a maple leaf by its five lobes. Canadians certainly should have no problem with this since it's on our flag. As for bigleaf maple (are you ready for this?), it has really big leaves, often 30 cm (12 in) wide. Mature trees reach 15 – 30 metres (50 – 100 ft) tall and trunk diameter at breast height ranges from 50 – 120 cm (20 – 48 in).

It ranges from latitudes 33° to 51° North and from the coast to about 300 km (186 miles) inland and from sea level to 2130 m (7000 ft) elevation. Large stands exist on Vancouver Island and on the western slopes of the Coast

Bigleaf Sugaring

Range in British Columbia. Stands can be found west of the Cascade Range in Washington and Oregon, and west of the Coast Range in California. Although the range extends south of the San Francisco Bay, the species is less common in that area.

Bigleaf maple is unique in regard to other maples in that leaf stalks secrete a milky sap when broken. More information regarding range, climate and soils can be found at http://forestry.about.com.

Young stand of bigleaf maple

Choosing the trees

Once you have identified your maples, it's time to choose the ones that should produce large amounts of sap. Some trees give prolific amounts of sap while others yield hardly a drop. Some trees are early season producers and others are late season producers. Age, size, form, crown, exposure and site may all play a role.

With this said, we have seemingly identical trees, side-by-side, that yield vastly different amounts of sap. Some of our maple trees leaf out weeks ahead of the trees next to them and lose their leaves weeks earlier. This may suggest that genetics makes a difference. Sounds like a good topic for a research project.

In testing the sugar content, we have found little vari-

This large tree didn't yield a drop of sap

ation between trees on the same day, but sugar content does fluctuate from day to day. Occasionally a tree will give a large amount of sap in a short period of time with lower sugar content; then, as the sap flow slows, the sugar content goes back to normal. (Another research project, you say?)

Even though we are tapping *trees*, most of us affectionately refer to our maple groves as the *sugarbush*. So let's head out to the sugarbush and select which trees we will tap.

Although we suggest what to look for when selecting your trees, you should experiment and find what works best for your site. Every rule for choosing ideal tapping trees has been broken with success. With that in mind, the following suggestions are general in nature so don't rule out a tree just because it doesn't fit the profile.

Age

Ideally we want a tree that is growing vigorously as

opposed to a mature tree. Bigleaf maples can live up to 300 years, but the growth often slows considerably after the first 50 – 100 years. We tap coppice stems as young as 10 years and single stem trees as young as 20 years.

By tapping a tree you are wounding it, and sap helps heal the wound. Older trees often have large branches break off and other large wounds. Instead of healing, the trees tend to compartmentalize these large wounds. This ability to compartmentalize damage may be why older, larger trees don't yield sap as well as younger ones.

Form

When a maple tree is cut down, the stump sends up many shoots. These are known as coppices. As the coppices grow vigorously from an existing root system, they can be ideal for sap collection. Later, in the section on managing your stand, we'll deal with coppice management.

Our experience has shown that coppices produce better earlier on in the season (December).

Single stem trees normally grow from seed, and since they don't have an existing root system on which to grow, they will be slower growing. In most cases we've found them to give better yields later on in the sugaring season (January) and coppices to produce better earlier in the season.

Ten-year old coppice stems from an existing stump

Tapping the trees 37

Size

Although we know many people that are successful at tapping large diameter trunks, we and many others have found trunk sizes from 10 - 45 cm (4 - 18 in) diameter the best sap producers for tapping coppices, and 25 - 45 cm (10 - 18 in) diameter best for single stem trees.

Crown

Normally you want to look for a tree that has a large crown. The crown is the branch structure. As said earlier, leaves are the sugar producers through photosynthesis, so it stands to reason that a large healthy crown will give good sap. Also said earlier, there are exceptions to every rule and we have taken great sap from younger trees with almost no crowns. In these exceptions the trees had lost their crowns due to breakage caused by the falling of an overmature neighbour tree.

Exposure

Back east people have to wait for the trees to thaw before sap can start flowing. For this reason, they suggest tapping trees with southern exposure that get sunlight much of the day. As temperature differences play a role in sap movement, it is probably wise to adopt this practice out west, even though freezing may not be a problem.

Site

Soils and moisture most likely play a role on sap quality and timing. Trees on wet sites will have their best flows earlier in the season than trees on drier sites. Maples like growing on creek banks, near seepage areas and by streams. They also grow in fairly dry sites, so their timing for sucking up huge amounts of water from the ground varies due to site conditions.

Soils may affect both syrup flavour and mineral content. Back east, maple syrup connoisseurs claim to taste the difference from one farm to another.

Avoid tapping trees next to a septic field or pig pen. Even a maple tree next to a cedar tree will be negatively affected by what's in the groundwater.

Summary

In general, if you have a choice, choose young healthy looking trees that are growing vigorously and have good exposure to the sun. However, this doesn't mean that older maples or trees in shady locations won't produce. The secret is to find which trees are your best producers and concentrate your energies on tapping them. You may find, as we do, that your top producers in November and December are not the top producers in January and February.

Drilling

Timing is everything. A hole drilled too soon before the sap runs will be a poor or nonproducer. When in doubt, snip a pencil sized branch or drill a test hole and see if there is a drip.

Tapping consists of drilling 11 mm (7/16 in) diameter holes about 10 - 13 cm (2 - 2.5 in) deep with a twist type bit. What you don't want to use is a flat, speed (spade) bit. A speed bit is more likely to jamb wood particles in the trees' sap vessels.

The hole should be drilled slightly uphill, so the sap will run out and so

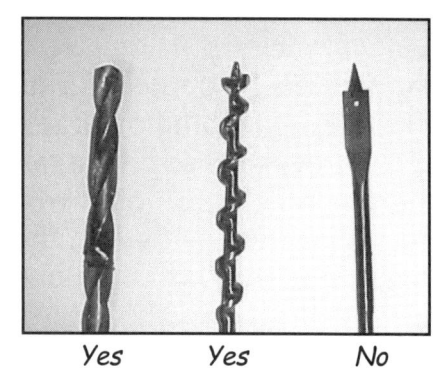

Yes   Yes   No

Tapping the trees

the tree can heal nicely without foreign matter running down the trunk and into the hole. For trees with thick bark, the depth of hole should be measured from the inside of the bark. Some eastern studies have shown that a 10 cm (4 in) deep hole will yield about 15% more sap.

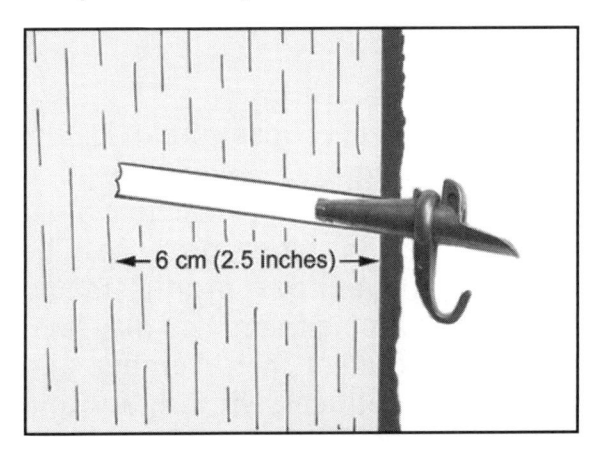

← 6 cm (2.5 inches) →

When drilling, watch your wood chip colour as you don't want to drill past the sapwood or tap a pocket of decayed wood. By wrapping tape around your drill bit at your desired depth, it's easy to know when to stop drilling. Once you reach the desired depth, keep twisting the drill clockwise and slowly pull it out, bringing as many loose woodchips with it as possible. Do not try to blow the chips out as this can contaminate the hole.

For years, most drilling was done with a brace and bit. Now, many people use cordless drills and even gasoline powered drills. Sanitizing the drill bit between trees is done by some people, but isn't a common practice. Sap will pick up flavour very easily and what you use to sanitize the bit could degrade the syrup's taste.

Although common practice is to tap on the sunny side of the tree, studies on eastern maples have reported that there is little bearing on which side or how high the tap hole is located. In the east they drill at a convenient height keeping in mind that the ground level will change as the snow melts. In our case, we like to drill within 60 - 90 cm (24 - 36 in) of the ground. As the sap rises from the roots, it has a shorter distance to travel. Some say the sugar content is higher further up the tree, but our limited testing of some tap holes done from a ladder, hasn't shown any difference in sugar content.

As you will be drilling the same trees at least twice each season, it's best to drill new holes a short distance over and up from the last holes. This way it will take a few years to work around the tree. Once around the tree, you can start low again or keep going up. The old holes will heal over within a year or so, complete with new bark.

Holes tend to start healing within four to six weeks, slowing the sap flow considerably. We have tried drilling first with a smaller diameter bit and then as the holes dry up, reaming the holes out with a larger bit. In our experiments this only worked for a day or two, and then the trees outsmarted us.

In the old days, people put a pellet of paraformaldehyde in each tap hole to keep it from becoming contaminated by bacteria. It wasn't a healthy practice for the trees or humans.

Healed tap hole from previous year

Tapping the trees

Sap collection and handling

Spiles

Spiles are available in plastic, cast aluminum and stainless steel. We recommend the plastic type with 7 mm (5/16 in) outlets. If used with tubing, these will help keep the tree holes from drying. Normally this system only requires re-tapping of holes about every five to six weeks as opposed to approximately every four weeks when using metal spiles.

Plastic spile

The metal spiles have a more traditional look and most come with a bucket hook that is removable. Plastic spiles are also available with bucket hooks.

Spiles are tapered and should be lightly tapped into the tree in order to provide a good seal. Sap enters the spile through a small hole. This hole can become plugged with sawdust or con-

Cast Aluminum spile

gealed sap and should be checked if a sap flow problem is suspected. Some people drill extra holes in the spiles. Spiles can be used year after year and are very inexpensive.

Plumbing

You want a sap collection system that keeps insects and rainwater out. You can create a closed sap collection system by using plastic spiles and tubing. Another benefit of using tubing is that you can use tees to plumb more than one stem into a container.

Vented spile at end of long run

When planning to tap several stems into a container, the first thing we do is create a level spot for the container to sit. Ideally this should be a shady spot, unless you plan to collect sap at least every other day.

Our standard practice is to cut a dropline of tubing about 30 cm (12 in) long and attach it to a tee on one end and a spile on the other. This is done before drilling the tap hole. The first tee will have a tube connected to the collection container. The next spile will have a similar dropline and tee, and the tap hole will be slightly higher than the first to give positive drainage. The tubing between the tees should be tight enough to prevent sap from pooling in a sag in the tube. If runs are long or more than four spiles are joined, using a tee or double outlet spile to vent the system is an option that some people choose.

If sap pools in the tubing and sits in the sun, it can start to ferment after a few days. Occasionally we don't

Spile, dropline and tee

Tag shows date of tapping

get our plumbing systems just right. By using see through tubing, we can see this potential problem. One simple solution is to lift the tubing by hand in order to drain it when collecting sap. As long as you drain these low spots every few days, you shouldn't have a problem.

Tees and tubing can be purchased at many hardware stores, but using the proper food-rated ones from a maple syrup supply store will not cost any extra and will be easier to work with. The only drawback is that the tubing has to be bought in 30 – 150 metre (100 to 500 ft) rolls. Ideally the tubing should be stiff and somewhat transparent. The stiffness is so you can plumb for positive drainage and the transparency is for cleaning. A word of caution is that on a cold day, once connected, the tubing doesn't easily come off the tees, so measure carefully.

Tees are available with a side plug and the plug can be used to hook your tubing to when emptying your sap containers. This helps to prevent the end of the tubing from getting dirty, as well as the possible loss of sap if there's a good flow at that moment.

Tee with plug

Containers

Four-litre milk jug hung on a spile

Some people use four-litre (1 US gal) milk jugs for sap collection containers. They cut a hole near the neck and hang them off the spile, eliminating the need for tubing. Our experience is that these are much too small and that they let in flies. It is also more labour intensive to collect sap from 30 small containers than it is from seven larger

Sap collection and handling

ones.

We've tried large commercial ice cream buckets with a tube hole drilled in through the side just below the lid. These buckets can be awkward to empty, but they are easy to clean.

Restaurant sized 16-litre (4 US gal) vegetable oil jugs are used by many for sap containers. These can usually be obtained free.

Clean by leaving the jugs upside down and slightly tilted in the sink to drain any remaining oil. Then add warm water and dish soap, put the cap back on, shake well and let sit. Repeat until all oil residue has been removed. Triple rinse. It is recommended to avoid using bleach, except at the end of the season, as it can adversely affect the flavour of the syrup.

16-litre vegetable oil jug connected to our top producing tree

Half of our jugs are used for transporting sap, the other half are used for collecting. Jugs used for collection are drilled with a 13 mm (1/2 in) hole in the cap. Usually we connect two to six spiles into one jug, although we have one tree that can sometimes fill a jug on its own in 24 hours.

Unfortunately the jugs can develope small holes after a season or two, and they can smell of rancid oil if not cleaned and rinsed thoroughly.

Large food grade plastic pails can also be used. They are easier to clean, but must have an easily removable lid for emptying. A hole for the tube is drilled into the side of the pail just below the lid. The advange of jugs over pails is that the jugs are clear and you can tell at a glance if the jug is near to overflowing.

Wine bags work well for sap collection and used ones can sometimes be obtained free, but they are difficult to clean. Those tapping for wine production find these bags preferable for collection. The main benefits of using wine bags is their ability to block out sunlight and to expand as the volume of sap in the bag increases so that there is only sap and not air in the bag. In general, these bags provide the benefit of an extremely closed system. They can be hung on the shady side of the tree using a piece of wire. The bag's plug is drilled to feed in the tubing. The 15 litre size works well, but can be a bit difficult to carry when full.

For those tapping in a big way, pipelines can be set up with a minimum 7% grade or a vacuum pump and fed into tanks. This requires a good stand of trees all in one area and a way to empty the tank for transport to your evaporator. In a perfect setup, the pipeline goes straight to the tank at the sugar shack.

Collection and storage

Both yeast and bacteria can affect sap. Because of this, sap needs to be collected often or it will spoil. Once the boiling process starts, all yeast and bacteria will be killed, but until then sap needs to be kept cool or frozen.

Ideally you should collect sap and boil it down every day, but few of us have time to do this. If temperatures are cool, you may be able to go as long as three days between collecting and boiling. We've successfully gone five days when weather is very cold. Tests back east have shown that syrup quality goes down if sap isn't processed after 24 hours and many set a limit at 48 hours.

If you are having good flows, you will have to collect every day or two so that the containers don't overflow and you will have to do the boiling almost daily to keep up.

The problem is when there isn't much flow. The temptation is to leave sap for another day or three. Ideally you should collect small amounts of sap and freeze it or pasteurize it by boiling for five minutes. After pasteurizing you can keep it in a cool place for a few more days. Studies have found that using UV lights will also work well in reducing yeast and bacteria counts.

In our first year of sugaring, we went out every afternoon with a pot just before dark to collect sap. As we were only running a three-spile operation, our biggest kitchen pot worked for collection. We'd gather what fit in the pot and start it boiling on the kitchen stove. Later we'd go back with a flashlight and get the rest of the sap.

As our operation grew, we started using a funnel and 16-litre vegetable oil jugs for collection. We found that the jugs at the trees

Oil jug with and without cardboard

should be rinsed at least weekly, so we progressed to a collection system of going out with clean jugs and swapping them with the jugs at the trees. This required a piece of maple branch or cork for closing the tube hole and a vehicle to carry all the jugs.

Collecting 100 or more litres a day (25 US gal) can be a lot of work and weight (100 kg / 220 lbs). The fewer times the sap is handled the better (for your back). With that in mind, a collection tank on a vehicle makes a lot of sense. The vehicle should then be able to be parked so that gravity can drain the tank to a second tank at the evaporator and that tank can also drain by gravity into your boiling pan. Somewhere in this process sap should be filtered.

Filtering

You can make good syrup without filtering, but you can make better syrup if you filter. If you don't filter, you'll have sediment in the bottom of your syrup jars. This sediment is mostly sugar sand (a.k.a. nitre), which consists of dissolved minerals, silica and bits of cellulose. You may have a few other organics in there too, depending on how clean and protected your collection and boiling process is. The syrup can be allowed to stand for a few weeks and then carefully poured off leaving the sediment in the bottom of the container. You can also clarify with egg—we'll get to that in the finishing section of this book.

Ideally, you should filter your sap before you begin boiling to remove any insects, tree needles, bits of leaves, bark, and other foreign matter. Inexpensive milk filters work well for this; you can buy them through your local feedstore or from a dairy supplier. Even better are the paper filters from a maple syrup supply store; they are very inexpensive, plus can be washed and reused many times. You can also

Sap collection and handling

use a piece of medium weight unbleached cotton cloth.

Once you get your sap boiled down to almost syrup, it should be filtered again while it is hot. Although paper filters can be used, Orlon or felt filters are more effective. These are much more expensive, but can be reused many times. They need to be wetted before using and even then they tend to soak up a lot of syrup.

For filtering syrup, we filter ours at about 55% sugar, using a paper filter on top of a cotton cloth filter and then return the syrup to boil until ready for bottling.

Filtering can be a slow procedure. It makes things easier if you can have a stepped work station so that you only need to tilt your container, instead of having to hold it while the sap or syrup slowly filters through into the next container or tank.

Filtering sap using paper filter cloth and a colander

Work station is stepped to allow pouring by tilting the sap jug

Evaporation & syrup making

Food Safety Practices

We recommend following good manufacturing and hygienic practices. The Ontario Ministry of Agriculture, Food, and Rural Affairs' website http://www.omafra.gov.on.ca/english/food/inspection/maple/maple_prod_food_safety.htm posts an excellent reference for General Principles of Food Hygiene, Composition and Labelling. Do not use aluminum pots or pans with lead solder.

Evaporators

Using the Rule of 86, you divide 86 by the percent of sugar in your sap. At 2% sugar, you divide 86 by 2 and get 43. That means you'll need 43 litres of sap to make one litre of syrup. The process is simple—you boil off 42 litres of water. That's a lot of airborne moisture to deal with. We've heard of a few occasions where it has worked well to remove wallpaper.

If you plan to do your evaporation inside, you will need to either be doing relatively small quantities or have a powerful ventilation system. If you don't have good mechanical ventilation, you can open windows and either dress warmly or crank up the heat. Better yet, do the first stages of evaporation outdoors.

Evaporator types
Kitchen stove—this is the easiest type of evaporator, especially for small quantities. We have a good exhaust hood and boil sap in two pots at a time. It certainly makes the house smell nice.
Hot plate—this makes a good, but somewhat slow evaporator and can be done outside as long as you don't electrocute yourself. A steamer pan can cover both burners if you have a two-element hot plate.

This pot was full when evaporation was started

Use a GFI outlet when working with electricity outdoors

Propane burner—these come in different sizes. A larger Btu model is desirable. We've found them a bit slower than the kitchen stove, but much faster than a hot plate. The downside is the cost of propane which works out to around $12 per litre of syrup.
Woodstove (in the home)—this method is very slow and you may only be able to evaporate 20 - 30 litres (4 - 6 US gal) of sap per day. At least you get to heat your home this way and will be warm enough to open lots of windows. You won't get much of a boil if using this method, and the syrup will be lighter coloured and milder tasting.
Woodstove (outside)—you can cut a hole in the top of an old woodstove for direct flame contact. Even better

Bigleaf Sugaring

efficiency will be gained if your pot or pan fits into the hole so heat isn't lost through the sides of the pan. Another solution is to make an insulating blanket to cover the sides of your pan or surround it with bricks. Expect to go through a lot of firewood as you will want to maintain a very hot fire.

Using a propane burner to do a small batch Sap is trickled in through a small hole in the coffee can

Homemade evaporator—you can build one of these wood fired units using concrete blocks, an old steel barrel, or other material. Oil fired models can be made from an old oil furnace. One of the more difficult aspects of building a homemade unit is finding a large enough pan.

Commercial evaporator—most problems can usually be solved by throwing enough money at them. If you are willing to spend $1000 or a lot more, you can have a commercial evaporator. The more basic models will evaporate about 20 litres (5 US gal) per hour. Most commercial units

Woodstove method (outside)

Evaporation & syrup making 53

are wood fired, efficient, and have some very handy features such as thermometer fittings and spigots.

Small wood-fired commercial evaporator

Boiling down

Your syrup will be flavoured very slightly by the type of fuel you use. Homemade evaporators that burn wood will almost always add a little wood smoke flavour due to smoke and ash contamination of the syrup. This isn't necessarily a bad thing. How hard you boil the sap will also be a factor in the taste and colour. Hard boiling is most common, and gives the syrup a caramelized taste and darker colour.

The pan or pot you use for boiling should have a large surface area, but does not need to be deep. For doing up to 50 litres of sap per day, smorgasbord-type steamer trays work well. These are available at most restaurant supply stores and are fairly inexpensive.

For efficient evaporation (unless you have a high powered heat source), you want to keep the sap level quite low in the pan, about 5 cm (2 in) deep. Basically, you want a strong boil if you are in a hurry to evaporate off the 42 litres of water to get your litre of syrup. This can be risky as the pot or pan can quickly go dry when there is only a small amount of sap left in the pan. This seemed to happen to us every year at first and we accidentally burned at least one batch. It's hard on the pan, a real mess to clean and very frustrating to waste that much sap.

As the sap level in the pan starts to get low you need to add more sap. If added too quickly it will kill the boiling action. We first attempted to solve this problem using a coffee can with a pinhole. The coffee can was perched on the edge of our pan. Every fifteen minutes or so, we'd fill the coffee can with sap and it would slowly dribble into the pan. We then went to using a larger scale of the same method using a 20-litre (5 US gal) plastic bucket that had a valve tapped into the bottom of the bucket and a hose running from it to our pan. The valve is adjustable to let

Bucket and valve provides a steady flow of sap at the same rate as evaporation occurs

the sap dribble in at the same rate as evaporation takes place.

This system worked well and required that we visit the sugar shack, which was just outside the back door, about every thirty minutes to feed the fire, check the sap flow, and skim off the foam. Foam contains solids that can impact the flavour of the syrup. A small, fine mesh wire strainer works well for skimming off foam. Having a bucket of clean water works well for cleaning the strainer.

If evaporating outside, you will need to have a roofed area as your sugar shack, since sugaring is done during the rainy season. This can be as simple as a small tarp over a wooden frame. The evaporated water will condense on your roof and rain down on you and everything in the sugar shack. To keep it from dripping back into the boiling sap (for sanitary reasons), you can hang an angled piece of sheetmetal or plexiglas high over the pan so that the condensation runs down the sheetmetal and drips miss the pan.

Finishing

The boiling process reduces the water content and kills any yeast or bacteria in the sap. Once enough boiling takes place to reduce the water content to around 50% (i.e. the sugar content is now 50%), it's wise to transfer your sap into a smaller pot. At that time we recommend you bring it inside to the kitchen stove where conditions will be more hygienic for finishing. You can judge if it's close to 50% by doing a bit of math comparing the volume to what you started with, for example; you started with 40 litres and you now have about two litres. A much easier and more enjoyable method is a taste test.

If you're working on a homemade or commercial wood-fired evaporator, you will need to put the fire out or let it burn down, so a little forethought is required. If your firebox door is large enough to get a shovel in, shoveling out the coals is quite an effective way to reduce the burn, but it can be messy and smoky. After a while you'll get the knack of knowing when to let the fire go out and you may let it

Skimming off foam produces better syrup

Evaporation & syrup making

get closer to 60% sugar before bringing it in for finishing.

For those running larger operations and wanting to do everything in the sugar shack, a commercial propane finishing unit is recommended.

Whether done large scale or on the kitchen stove, depth of syrup for finishing is very important. Many of us have learned this one the hard way. We find it's best to transfer our "almost syrup" into a pot the correct size to give about 15 cm (6 in) depth of product. Filter while doing this transfer. Using a paper milk filter works but isn't quite as effective in reducing sugar sand. Filtering can go slow if the filter clogs up, so we now use a paper filter on top of a medium weight unbleached cotton cloth and that seems to work much better. For those who don't want to filter, you can clarify with egg or use gravity to settle out sugar sand (nitre).

After boiling for a length of time on the stove, your sap should have the taste of slightly watered-down syrup. Syrup depth will most likely have been reduced to under 8 cm (3 in), so it would be wise to transfer your syrup to a smaller diameter pot. During this transfer is the last time we filter our syrup. We don't filter when bottling as our filter cloth is not sterile.

When starting off with small quantities of sap, you may not have enough syrup to safely do the finishing. By freezing your small quantities of partially reduced sap, you can save up a sufficient amount to make finishing easier.

Another option is to finish in a 200 - 250° F oven.

Sugar sand

Sugar sand is caused when maple sugar crystalizes around mineral particles. Letting syrup cool and reheating seems to increase the amount of sand. Filtering or using settling to remove sand allows the syrup to cool off and then reheating adds to the sand problem.

During the the tapping season the amont of sand can vary greatly depending on the amount of malic acid in the sap. Syrup that is taken past 66.5% sugar will have larger amounts of sand.

At times the sand will form on the bottom of your finishing pot and create miniature volcanic eruptions. If this happens, transfer to a clean pot.

If you do end up with large quantities of sugar sand, place in a jar and let it settle for a few days for the syrup to rise to the top. Some people cook with the sand, some add water and boil, then add the water to their next boil-down. Another option is to add vodka and/or brandy to the sand, let it stand for a week, then pour off and enjoy.

Too sweet, this jar has a layer of sugar crystals at the bottom

Calling it syrup

The final step to calling it syrup is reaching 66.5% sugar. Syrup with less than 65% sugar can grow a black mould and above 68%, sugar will crystalize in your product. Ironically, mould doesn't always hurt the taste. When this happened to us in our early days, we filtered and then reboiled the syrup and it was still good.

Many people will try to determine 66.5% by taste. Some people will even keep a bit of store-bought maple syrup on hand to compare sweetness. A Brix sugar refractometer is an accurate and easy way of testing sugar content and only uses a couple drops of syrup.

You can purchase a sugar (syrup) hydrometer for about

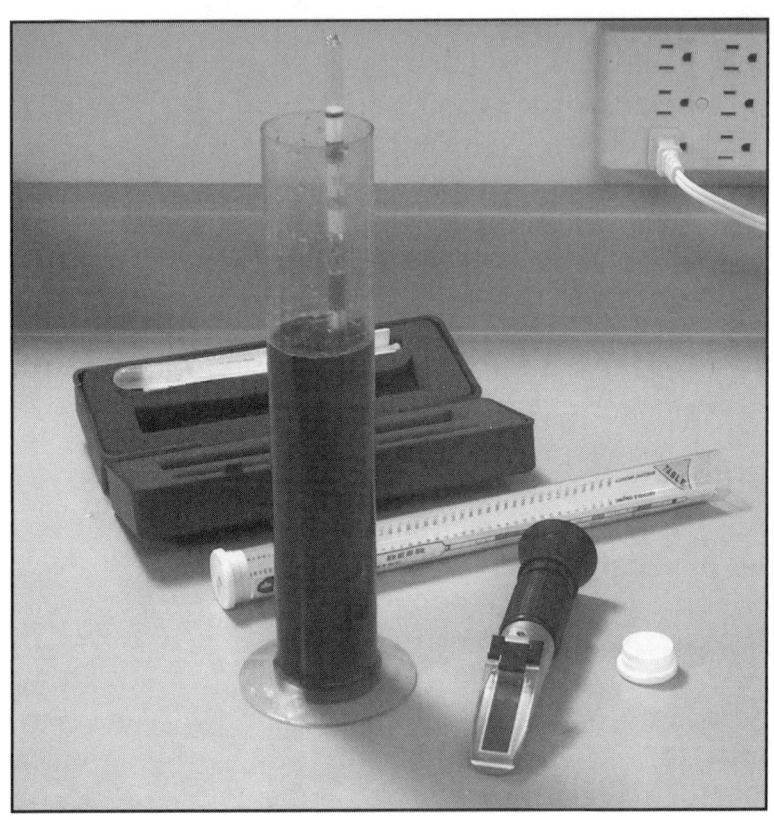

Hydrometer and refractometer—used for suger testing

$15. Wine and beer hydrometers will work for measuring the sugar content of sap, but most won't go high enough for syrup. Hydrometers work by measuring specific gravity. The specific gravity of 66.5% syrup is between 1.32 and 1.33. If you buy a syrup hydrometer you won't have to deal with specific gravity, but you will have to correct for temperature. You also have to be very gentle when lowering the hydrometer into the syrup. If it bobs down, the glass will get coated with syrup adding weight and changing the reading.

The most common method of determining 66.5% is by measuring maximum temperature. You start this process by boiling some water. In theory, water boils at 100° C (212° F), but the same atmospheric pressure fluctuations that affect sap flow will also change the boiling temperature of water. Once you get water to a hard boil, you can't get it any hotter. If you add more heat, it just turns to gas quicker. Sugar on the other hand will not evaporate so you can get sugar hotter than boiling water.

We use a candy thermometer and place enough water in a pot so the end of the thermometer is well submerged, but not too close to the bottom of the pot to give a false reading. We allow the water to boil for at least five minutes, then take a reading. Our readings have been anywhere from 99° – 102° C. Next we transfer the thermometer to the pot of boiling syrup. Syrup is 66.7% sugar once its boiling temperature reaches 4.1° C (7° F) higher than the temperature of boiling water.

Using temperature to determine sugar content

Once you become an old hand at finishing, you can tell when it's syrup by the way bubbles behave. As it reaches 66.5%, the bubbles will get smaller and become darker in colour. Using a pancake flipper or other large flat cooking utensil you can dip the syrup and watch it flow off the utensil, checking for an apron to form. This is easier to see with cold syrup than with hot.

Making syrup is like making wine, many things affect quality of taste. You can control some factors such as cleanliness, using food-grade sap collecting supplies, filtration, amount of skimming and your evaporation methods. Other factors such as season, weather and sap flow are out of your hands. We occasionally line up different batches we and others have made and have tasting parties. Just like wine, we each have favourites and not everyone's is the same.

A WORD OF CAUTION: Your sap/syrup will be a very hot liquid, so be careful!! Things move fast at the end and many people accidentally burn and ruin all their hard work. It's best to finish off a large quantity of syrup rather than a small one. It is recommended, if necessary, to store up small quantities of partly reduced sap (approx. 50% sugar) until you have enough to do a larger batch.

Bottling and storage

Finished syrup should be poured into hot sterile bottles while it's still boiling hot. Seal tightly and tip upside down for 30 seconds to make sure the lid is sterilized. We use a stainless steel coffee urn. The syrup is placed in the urn about an hour before bottling to let the sand settle out.

Glass syrup bottles are best for syrup. They can be expensive to get shipped to your location. If you live near a large town, you might be able to find an affordable source of these without them having to be shipped to you. If you are selling your product to the high-end gift market, having a nice bottle and label is important.

Metal cans and plastic jugs are very affordable and quite durable. The traditional maple syrup ones are not see-through, but are designed for hot packing. Both metal and plastic containers can affect the syrup flavour.

Instead of bottling, an easier method is to freeze or can your syrup. Evaporate the sap down to at least 60% sugar, place in canning jars, then can it using a water

Syrup containers are available in metal, glass and plastic

bath. This will allow particles to settle to the bottom of the jar during storage. At a later date you can gently pour off the clear syrup, finish to 65% and bottle.

Syrup should be refrigerated after opening.

Syrup grading rules

Most of the syrup made from bigleaf maple will be cooking grade. Compared to sugar maple, bigleaf maple takes more sap to produce the same amount of syrup. Because of this our syrup is darker. This isn't necessarily a bad thing, because it means our syrup also has more flavour. When used as a gourmet cooking ingredient this extra flavour is highly desirable.

Traditionally, syrup has been graded by colour. Canada and the US have separate but similar grading systems and within these two countries, Quebec and

Evaporation & syrup making

Vermont have their own systems. Although colour is the primary criteria, objectionable odour or taste, cloudiness and other factors are also part of the grading.

North America seems to be a society that in the past preferred light coloured foods: white flour, white bread, white rice, and white sugar. This seems to carry over to maple syrup, the lighter and more delicate the taste, the higher the grade. Full-bodied stronger tasting syrups are graded lower and are sometimes referred to as *cooking grade*.

In Canada, Grades are No. 1, 2 and 3. Grade No. 1 is divided into three subgrades, extra light, light and medium. Grade No. 2 is amber. Grade No. 3 is dark (i.e. darker than amber). These five colour classes can be measured using a spectrophotometer.

Colour Class	**% of Light Transmission**
Extra Light	75.0 or greater
Light	from 60.5 to 74.9
Medium	from 44.0 to 60.4
Amber	from 27.0 to 43.9
Dark	less than 27.0

All maple syrup must be labeled to show the following
- Type of product (i.e. maple syrup)
- Ingredients (i.e. maple syrup)
- Volume units for maple syrup
- Name and address of packer/producer
- Country of Origin (where applicable)

When shipping more than 100 litres at a time out of British Columbia, the label must also show the grade and colour class.

Advertisements for maple syrup must also state the

grade and volume of the maple syrup as prominently as the price when a price is quoted. Container sizes over 125 ml are regulated and restricted to 250 ml, 375 ml, 500 ml, 540 ml, 750 ml, 1 litre, 1.5 litre and any multiple of 1 litre. Containers of five litres or less must be new and containers are to be filled to at least 90% of their capacity.
In the US, Grade A and Grade B designations are used. Both grades are further divided into light amber, medium amber and dark amber. Grade B is for reprocessing only, and not for consumer sized packaging.

Substances that can degrade a syrup include chlorine, detergent, non-food grade paint, metal, plastic, filters, defoamer, yeast, mould, burnt nitre and buddy (season). Colour can be measured using coloured glass samples or liquid samples. Both Canadian and US grading kits are available from maple syrup supply stores and range in price from $25 – $500.

Evaporation & syrup making

Flavour Wheel for Maple Products

It has long been recognized that maple syrups have a wide range of taste even within the same grade category. Each farm can have a distinct taste to its syrup and different batches will even have different tastes within the same farm.

Agriculture and Agri-Food Canada recently developed a flavour wheel for maple products to help people describe the different flavours. The tasting procedure for using the wheel is much like wine tasting. The wheel has a number of flavour categories, with each flavour divided into subflavours. The intent is to be able to help the consumer find the product that best appeals to their palate.

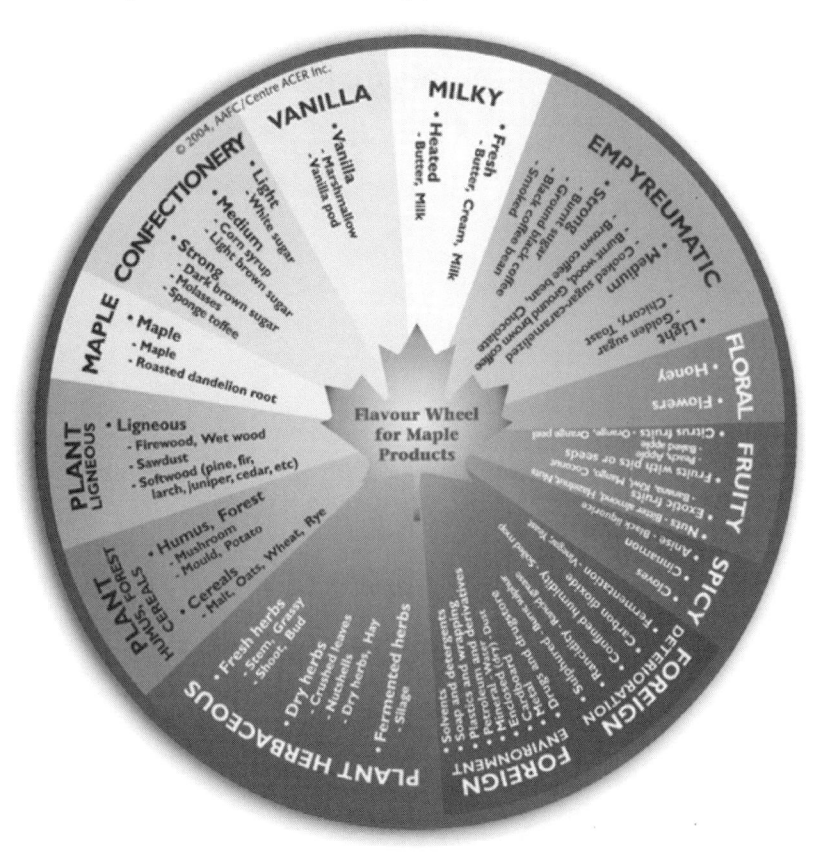

Bigleaf Sugaring

Tasting Maple Syrup
(Excerpt from Flavour Wheel for Maple Products)
Although professional tasters require extensive training, you can sharpen your tasting skills by following these steps:
1. First, smell the syrup by taking three quick sniffs. Make a mental note of your impression. Next, take a small sip of the syrup and swirl it around in your mouth. It is a good idea to spit it out if you can. Take about a minute to concentrate on the full range of flavours.
2. Try to associate the flavour with your own experience (for example, the aroma from a bag of marshmallows).
3. If possible, share your reaction with others, as this often helps trigger memory association. Once you have identified what you think characterizes the taste, memorize the sensation and the name for it (for example, vanilla).
4. Finally, try to assess the degree of intensity (e.g. mild, medium or strong).

Reproduced with the permission of the Minister of Public Works and Government Services Canada, 2003

http://www.agr.gc.ca/maple_wheel

Steam rising from a commercial evaporator at the UBC Research Farm in Oyster River

Ending the season

Bud burst

When to call it quits

In theory you can continue tapping until bud burst, in other words, until the flower buds start to open. This usually occurs some time in March. As the bud growth rapidly accelerates, the sugar percentage of the sap and the quality of flavour decreases.

In our own experiences, the sugar and flavour decreases are only minimal, but the sap yield slows down to next to nothing, making it more work than it's worth to continue tapping. Our sugarbush is located on Vancouver Island on a warm south facing hillside, and depending on weather we usually stop tapping some time during the last two weeks of February.

Pulling the taps

Spiles don't always want to leave the tree easily. Often a twist and pulling motion will be all that's needed, but you may run into some pretty tight spiles. You can buy a spile puller for about $15. We used to use the claw of a hammer, but have switched over to spile pullers as there's less likely hood of damaging the spile or tree. The design of spile will also determine what you can use as a puller, as some spiles have little to pry against.

Cleaning the equipment

Spiles, tubing and containers will need to be thoroughly cleaned and rinsed before you store them away for the season. As you are dealing with a food product that easily picks up flavour, you'll need to be careful in what you use to kill bacteria (mould and yeast growths), and remove calcium and other mineral build-ups. Soap and bleach can both flavour the syrup.

All equipment should be cleaned at the end of the season

The commercial maple syrup industry uses the same type of products as the milk industry for disinfecting equipment. The cleaner comes in two forms, foaming and non-foaming. The non-foaming is more expensive and is used in situations where it is pumped through tubing. Because these are acid-based products, shipping can be quite expensive, so buying through a local dairy supplier may be the most affordable solution.

The product we purchased through our local dairy supplier is Della-Pan. It's a liquid biodegradable acid produced for the sugarbush industry and is designed to be diluted with warm water at a ratio of 3:100. Safety protection should be worn when using this type of product.

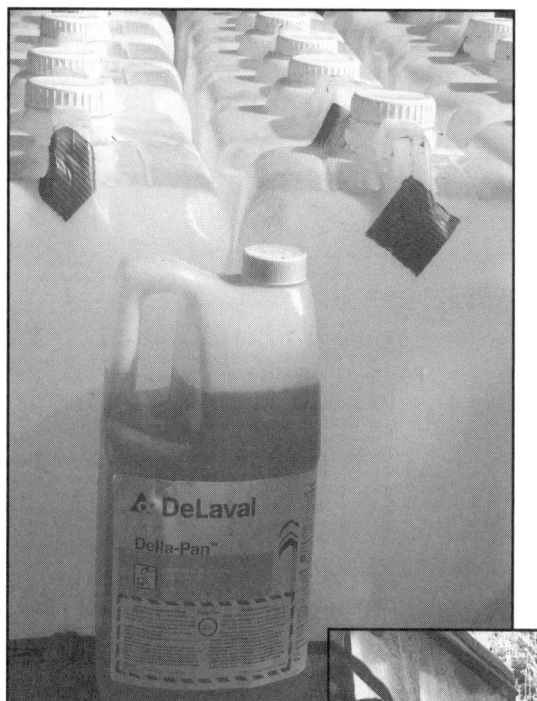

Personally, we try to use as few chemicals as possible. Our cleaning method is to leave our spiles attached to the tubing. For each set of connected spiles, tees and tubing, we insert one spile into a garden hose (just like inserting it into a tap-hole) and we turn on the water for a minute or so. This blasts water through all the tubing, tees and spiles. We leave the spile, dropline and tees connected as these are labeled and will be reused next year at the same locations. Any equip-

Using a garden hose to pressure wash spiles, tees and tubing

Ending the season

ment that doesn't look clean enough gets soaked in a Della-Pan solution.

We have a weeping willow tree growing beside our sugar shack and discovered that willow branches do a great job of scouring the inside walls of the tubing, removing sap residue and mineral deposits.

At end of season our collection jugs are filled with a mild bleach solution and left to soak for a week or two. After this presoaking, each jug is emptied then sprayed with a jet stream of water from a hose. The exterior of the bucket is scrubbed and rinsed to remove any remaining traces of soil then placed into a large tub filled with a water/bleach solution.

Jugs get scrubbed inside and out then triple rinsed in another tub which is filled with clean water.

After cleaning and triple rinsing, they are given a final inspection for any signs of residue, then placed upside down on a rack to drain. After draining, jugs are stacked on their side to air dry. Then they are transferred to clean, dry storage shelves until the next season.

Caps are also sanitized, scrubbed, triple rinsed and air dried before being put into storage.

Containers need to "breathe" during storage so ensure that either the jug or cap has a tube hole drilled in it, or leave the caps off.

As most of your tapping equipment is made from plastic, it should be stored away from the sun's harmful U-V rays.

Tree stand management

Habitat

As mentioned earlier in this book, bigleaf maple has a range from southern British Columbia to southern California. Its range seems to be governed by temperature, -20° C is its lower limit. In British Columbia it grows from sea level to about 350 m (1150 ft). Further south it grows at higher elevations, and at its extreme southern range it grows between 915 and 2135 m (3000 – 7000 ft). Its range is almost always within 300 km (186 mi) of the Pacific Ocean.

Bigleaf maple favours moist sites and riparian areas, such as springs and seepage areas, and river, creek and stream banks. It can tolerate flooding for short durations. It isn't a pioneer species and doesn't tend to grow in disturbed sites or in clear-cut areas (except from existing stumps). Seldom does it grow in pure stands; it seems to prefer partial shade and is often found growing in a mixed stand of Douglas-fir.

Root systems are shallow and wide. This type of root system functions well for wet sites. Seedlings can grow up to two metres (6.5 ft) per season, but growth rates are very site specific and may only reach 2.5 cm (1 in) in height during a season.

Bigleaf maples are soil builders and their leaves contain high levels of potassium and calcium, plus other soil building nutrients. The trees prefer a moist, deep gravelly soil, but will grow on shallow rocky soils.

Tree health

We've had several larger maples and many smaller ones growing in the wrong place. Not the wrong habitat, but the wrong place for our plans. Trying to kill a bigleaf maple without actually digging up the stump is quite difficult. The obvious method is cutting down the tree and then stripping off the new sprouts each year. After a couple of years of this, we tried burning a stump with no success in killing it. We've tried girdling the trees, but that wasn't effective either.

The fact that these trees are hard to kill says a lot about how resilent they really are. Unlike their eastern cousins, bigleaf maple can take a lot of abuse so tapping doesn't seem to bother them. The exception to this is that tapping may affect the lumber quality when and if the tree finally gets harvested for milling.

Decay, caused by invasion of fungi, accounts for much of the defect in bigleaf maples. This is often found as butt rot in overmature trees, but can be found in younger trees where stem and branch wounds become invasion ports for wood rotting fungi. Tapping the trees creates an opening

Decay caused by injury

for fungi. Fortunately, most of this type of rot only travels downward. Trees growing off-site will be more easily stressed and therefore more susceptible to fungi than those growing in ideal habitat.

Spacing the stand

Few studies have been done on the effects of stand spacing, but the research that has been done recommends that stands should be kept somewhat dense. If grown only as a sugarbush operation, trees should be kept in clumps to allow easy connections of collection systems. Stems can be as close as a metre (3 ft) apart or even closer.

When grown for millable timber, the objective is a tree that grows straight up with limited branching. Spacing too far apart not only increases branching, but too much sun slows height development. If no competition exists on one side of a tree, it will often develop a lean in that direction, which will cause a mixture of tension and compression in the stem (trunk). This compressed and stressed wood fibre results in lumber bowing and warping during drying.

When growing for lumber as your final product, trees in pure stands should be planted or spaced about two metres apart, and when they reach about six metres tall (20 ft), they should be spaced to about four or five metres apart (13 – 16 ft). This may sound easy, but nature will have its own ideas as to tree location and you may have some trees closer together and others spaced further apart than this recommended distance. These numbers are very general and spacing requirements may differ depending on slope aspect, moisture, elevation and other factors.

Coppice control

When bigleaf maple trees are felled, the stumps coppice, producing many shoots. These coppice stems can grow 5 metres (16 ft) in height over as little as three years. They start out using the existing root structure of the stump, but as the stump rots, the coppices develop their own root systems. Because the stump does rot, coppices growing high above ground level will have poor attachment and will often fall over when they become too top heavy.

Ideally, after felling the trees, stumps should be cut off close to ground level. A single stump may produce up to 60 shoots, and these should be thinned when they are about three or four years old, down to two to six stems (depending on stump size). This should be done mid-summer, as summer pruning tends to discourage growth. In about 50% of the stumps that we have treated, the energy gets channeled into the remaining stems instead of growing more stems. The other 50% require additional coppice treatments about three years later.

Typical coppiced stump

Coppices should be well spaced and have an almost ground level attachment to the stump. Normally we leave those growing on the perimeter of the stump. If the stumps are cut low enough, coppices growing near the centre of the stumps will also be good choices to leave.

Harvesting for lumber

Depending on the site, bigleaf maple will have a 25 to 70 year rotation when grown for lumber. Saw logs are usually a minimum 25 cm (10 in) diameter and there is a high amount of firewood produced. As much of the lumber is for the woodworking market, lumber length can be as short as one metre (3 ft). Unusual grain patterns often bring higher value, and some patterns such as fiddleback, flame and quilted can be very valuable.

Coppices reduced to three stems

Although there is a market for bigleaf maple logs, prices are low. In many cases a portable bandsaw mill can be brought on site to mill logs. You should cut your boards about 3 mm (1/8 in) thicker than the rough size you want due to saw kerf and shrinkage, and 10 mm (3/8 in) thicker than the finished (after planing) size you want.

Milling bigleaf maple with a bandsaw (Katherine age 6)

Ideally, logs for milling should be from trees that don't have much lean. Lumber will be more stable if the logs are allowed to season for two or three years before milling, but logs can also be milled immediately after felling. When seasoning logs, full sun is to be avoided. It's best if logs can be kept off the ground, but this isn't too important unless they are lying in a wet area.

Lumber can be air dried (seasoned) in a shady or partially sunny location, but shouldn't be exposed to full sun. Edge trims can be used to sticker the lumber. Recommended sticker spacing is about 60 cm (24 in) apart. Ends of the boards should be painted with a thick finish to allow for even drying in order to minimize end checking (splitting).

We do most of our drying in sheds, but have successfully used a tent-shaped white tarp that stops about 30 cm (12 in) from the ground. We usually lay a plastic ground cover under the pile to prevent ground-source moisture from slowing drying. Lumber will usually take one summer per 25 mm (1 in) thickness to dry.

    We sometimes season logs up to three years to allow a fungus to work its way through the wood. This produces lumber with black lines running in interesting patterns. The term for this is spalted maple and is a favourite for some woodworkers. If you leave the log too long, you end up with rot and worthless lumber.

Lumber being air-dried
Stickers (in foreground) are placed between each row at 60 cm (24 in) apart

Cooking with liquid gold

Appendix A—Recipes

Cooking with maple sap and syrup is not only nutritious; it's also a real joy. If you do an Internet search for maple syrup recipes, you'll find thousands including free maple syrup cookbooks. You'll find many of our favourites at http://www.bcforestmuseum.com/.

Maple sap

Maple sap can be used in lieu of water for most recipes. We keep a jug of sap handy for kitchen use during the tapping season. Sap only keeps for a few days, so what's left of this jug's contents gets added to the evaporator every other day and we refill the jug with fresh sap. We also freeze sap for use in cooking during the summer.

Bread

Use unpasteurized sap instead of water for your bread machine recipes and you can expect to get a better rise. Sap contains natural yeasts that complement bread yeast.

Rice

Use 1.5 to 2 cups of sap per cup of rice (amount depends on cooking method and type of rice). Rice will have a bit of sweetness and a slight maple flavour.

Soup

Use sap in place of water for making any type of soup. Soup will have an extra heartiness. Potato soup using sap as a base is one of our favourites. We often add slightly more sap than the amount of water called for in the recipe.

Stew

This is a real wintertime favourite around our place, especially with dumplings.

    1.5 - 2 lbs stew meat, cut into large bite-sized cubes
    2 tablespoons shortening
    1 teaspoon Worcestershire sauce
    1 - 2 cloves garlic
    2 medium or 1 large onion, chopped in large chunks
    1 green or other colour bell pepper, chopped in large chunks
    4 - 6 large carrots, cut in large bite-sized pieces
    4 potatoes pared and quartered
    2 bay leaves
    1 tablespoon salt
    1 teaspoon sugar
    ½ teaspoon paprika
    Dash allspice or cloves
    Gravy
    Dumplings (optional)

In a thick-bottomed pot or Dutch oven, brown meat in shortening. Add 2 ¼ cups of hot sap, Worcestershire sauce, garlic, onion and spices. Cover and cook on stovetop for about 90 minutes. Stir occasionally. Remove bay leaves and add potatoes, green pepper and carrots. Cook for 30 to 45 additional minutes (until potatoes and carrots are tender).

Gravy

Skim off fat, then drain liquid into a microwave safe bowl. Ideally you should have about 1 ¾ cups of liquid. Add sap if needed. Mix ¼ cup of water and two tablespoons of flour until well blended and add to the liquid in the microwave-safe bowl. Microwave and stir every 60 seconds until thick. Once thick, return gravy to stew mixture.

Dumplings (optional)
Sift a cup of flour with 2 teaspoons of baking powder and ½ teaspoon of salt. In a separate bowl, mix ½ cup of milk together with 2 tablespoons of vegetable oil. Make a well in the flour mixture and add the milk mixture. Stir until just moistened and drop by spoon on top of the stew-gravy mixture. Cover and cook over low heat until done (will be somewhat doughy).

Tea
Sap can be used for making many hot beverages. Some favourites include; mint tea, lemon tea, green tea and licorice tea.

Maple syrup
Bigleaf maple syrup has a stronger flavour than eastern maple syrup. For some people the extra flavour may be a bit too much for use as pancake syrup. This extra flavour allows bigleaf maple syrup to excel as a gourmet cooking ingredient. In many cases, a small amount of syrup goes a long way.

Ice Cream Topping
Pour a small amount of bigleaf maple syrup over vanilla ice cream. Not only is this a simple dessert, it's a great way of introducing people to the great taste of bigleaf maple syrup. We occasionally get together with other syrup producers and have tasting parties using vanilla ice cream. Ice cream is a great medium to use to bring out the true flavour of maple syrup.

Glaze

A bigleaf maple syrup glaze can be made to coat vegetables such as baby carrots. It's also great on smoked meats such as ham or on salmon. Another use for a maple glaze is as a dessert topping for cheesecakes and other goodies. Glaze recipes can run from simple to complex.

Basic Glaze

Dissolve 1 ½ teaspoons of cornstarch in ½ cup of water. Add ¼ cup of bigleaf maple syrup. Microwave, stirring every 2 – 3 minutes, until thickened. For a sweeter glaze, use equal portions of water and syrup.

Spicy Meat Glaze

Mix and apply to meat during the last 15 minutes of cooking.
    ½ cup maple syrup
    1 ½ tablespoons mustard seed
    3 tablespoons Balsamic vinegar
    3 tablespoons prepared mustard
    1 ½ tablespoon dry mustard

Overnight Maple French Toast

(Courtesy of Peggy Kolosoff of Kiwi Cove Lodge)
    2/3 cup packed brown sugar
    ½ cup bigleaf maple syrup
    1 tablespoon butter
    10 – 12 slices French bread, cut 1" thick
    4 eggs
    1 ½ cups milk
    1 teaspoon vanilla
    1/8 teaspoon salt
    Sliced strawberries and powdered sugar for garnish

Oil a 9" X 13" Pyrex pan. In medium saucepan, heat brown sugar, syrup and butter stirring constantly. Pour syrup mixture into the Pyrex pan. Arrange bread slices over the syrup mix. In large bowl combine eggs, milk, vanilla and salt. Whisk till smooth. Pour evenly over bread. Cover, refrigerate overnight. Bake uncovered in preheated 350° F oven for 30 – 35 minutes (till lightly browned)
Top with strawberries and icing sugar before serving.

Salad Dressing (our favourite)
 ¼ cup bigleaf maple syrup
 ¼ cup cranberry juice or cocktail
 ¼ cup red wine vinegar
 ½ cup vegetable oil
 1 teaspoon Dijon mustard

Appendix B—Equipment Sources

Equipment suppliers

http://www.thebeestore.ca
Bees 'n Glass
6456 Cowichan Lake Road
Lake Cowichan, BC   V0R 2G0
Phone: (250) 749-3800
Toll free: 1-877-256-3800

http://www.buckerfields.org
Buckerfield's Farm & Garden Stores
Duncan: (250) 748-8171
Nanaimo: (250) 753-4221
Parksville: (250) 248-3243
Saanich: (250) 652-9188

http://www.dominiongrimm.ca (Canada & USA)
Dominion and Grimm
Phone: (514) 351-3000
Toll free: 1-877-676-1914
USA Callers: (801) 524-9625

http://www.atkinsonmaple.com
Atkinson Maple Syrup Supplies
RR 1, 2907 Highway 11
Oro Station, Ontario, Canada   L0L 2E0
Phone: (705) 487-3331
Fax: (705) 487-0460

http://www.leaderevaporator.com/
Leader Evaporator Company
25 Stowell Street
St. Albans, Vermont, USA 05478
Phone: (802) 524-4966 or (802) 524-3931
Fax: (802) 527-0144

Other sources of information

http://www.omafra.gov.on.ca/english/food/inspection/maple/maple_prod_food_safety.htm
Ontario Ministry of Agriculture, Food, and Rural Affairs
Food Safety Practices for the Production of Maple Syrup

http://www.bcforestmuseum.com/
BC Forest Discover Centre

http://cle.royalroads.ca/
Royal Roads University
Centre for Livelihoods and Ecology

http://www.fs.fed.us/pnw/pubs/rn181.pdf
(1970 – 1971 Oregon Bigleaf Maple study into harvesting sap for syrup)

http://ohioline.osu.edu/for-fact/0036.html
Hobby maple syrup production (for eastern Sugar Maple)

http://forestry.about.com/library/silvics/blsilacemac.htm
(Silviculture)

http://infobasket.gov.bc.ca/
(Good source for agroforestry information)

http://www.blmaple.net (author's website)

Appendix C—Glossary of Terms

Apron—a sheet-like formation when *syrup* is dripped from a flat metal utensil. It is caused by having a high level of viscosity.
Brix—a scale for measuring the relative density of a sugar solution. Developed by Adolf F. Brix.
Boiling down—(a.k.a. boiling off) the process of removing water from *sap* by boiling.
Bud burst—the opening of the maple flower buds in early spring.
Buddy—an unpleasant taste or flavour given to the *sap* that is associated with *bud burst*.
Cambium layer—the inner layer of the bark, through which sugar and food travels down from the leaves to mix with water and minerals from the roots in order to form *sap*. The *cambium layer* is part of the *phloem*. The division of these cells will create diameter growth of the tree through formation of new wood cells (xylem) and also inner bark.
Checking—cracks caused by drying that may only go part way through a board or may occur at the ends of a board (end *checking*).
Clarify with egg—the process of using egg white to remove cloudiness from maple *syrup*
Coppice—the process of sending up new stems from an existing stump or root system. The name given shoots that sprout from stump level.
Crown—the foliage and branch structure of a tree. Crown is measured in spread and in proportion to the amount of trunk it stems from. 50% crown would suggest that the branches extend from the top of the tree midway down the trunk.

Dormant season—the season when the leaves are off the trees (usually fall and winter).
Dropline—tubing from the spile to a tee or container.
Evaporator—a device for boiling *sap* in order to remove water to create *syrup*. Also known as an arch.
Flavour Wheel—developed by Agriculture and Agri-Food Canada, this chart helps people to describe the taste of a particular batch of maple *syrup*.
Filtering—the use of a permeable membrane (e.g. milk filter, cotton cloth, Orlon) to remove undesired organics from *sap* and *syrup*.
Food-Rated—a designation given to materials that are safe to use in food production and storage.
Girdling—to remove a strip of bark (including *cambium layer*) around the circumference of a stem in order to kill the tree or slow its growth.
Heartwood—the centre woody portion of the stem. These cells are nonliving and often darker in colour than *sapwood*.
Hydrometer—a device for measuring specific gravity of liquids in order to determine sugar content. Requires correction for temperature.
Managed forest—a term used in British Columbia for registered private forestland that falls under a management commitment. Similar to what is known as a woodlot in other parts of Canada and the USA.
Maple sugaring—the process of tapping trees and making *syrup* and/or other edible maple products.
Maple water—a name sometimes used for *sap*. See *sap*
Nitre—see *sugar sand*.
Non-Timber—non-log or non-lumber tree products such as floral greens and maple *syrup*.
Refractometer—a device for measuring sugar content using the refraction of light. Does not require correction for temperature.

Pan—a container for boiling *sap*. Normally this container is shallow and has a large surface area.
Phloem—layer of tree tissue between the bark and *sapwood* through which sugar and food travel from the leaves to the stems and roots.
Photosynthesis—the conversion of water and carbon dioxide to sugar and oxygen using sunlight. Photosynthesis mainly occurs through leaves, but also takes place through thin bark.
Respiration—the opposite of *transpiration*. The tree burns some sugar and produces energy and CO_2. Normally there is only about one tenth as much *respiration* as there is *transpiration*.
Rule of 86—a rough calculation of *sap* to *syrup* ratio based on *sap* sugar content. 86 divided by the sugar percent of *sap* equals the number of *sap* units needed to make one unit of *syrup* (i.e. 86/2% = 43 therefore at 2% sugar it should require 43 litres of *sap* to make one litre of syrup).
Sap—a water like substance that consists of water and minerals from the roots plus sugar and protein from the leaves. *Sap* travels upward through the *sapwood*.
Sapwood—the light coloured wood nearest the bark. The inner part of the stem is the *heartwood*.
Spile—a tapered pipe or fitting used to drain the taphole into tubing or a container.
Stem—a trunk that will support branches.
Sticker—a thin strip of wood used to separate boards or planks while drying.
Sugarbush—a slang term for a stand of maples that get tapped for making *syrup*.
Sugaring—see *Maple Sugaring*.
Sugar sand—minerals, silica, and cellulose that settles out of maple *syrup*. Also know as *nitre*.

Sugar shack—a building or shed used for boiling *sap* to make *syrup*.
Syrup—when *sap* is boiled to a point that the sugar content is 66.5%, it can then be called *syrup*.
Tap—to drill a hole in the stem of a tree in order to collect *sap*.
Tapping season—the period of time when the *sap* flow is plentiful, sweet and good tasting. Often extends through much of the *dormant season*.
Tee—a fitting for joining three pieces of tubing. Tees are normally used to connect several spiles to one container.
Transpiration—the process of pushing *sap* to the leaves to convert water and carbon dioxide into sugar and oxygen through *photosynthesis*.
Tubing—flexible pipe used to connect spiles to the collection containers.
Wolf tree—a tree with a very large branch structure whose footprint takes up the growing space where many trees could grow. A wolf tree takes up more space than its merchantable value warrants.
Woodlot—in British Columbia a woodlot is a licensed piece of publicly owned forestry land managed by a private company.

Appendix C—Glossary of Terms

Index

A
apron 61, 88

B
bacteria 47, 70
bigleaf maple
  air drying lumber 78
  crop rotation 77
  decay 74
  habitat 73
  identifying 34
  leaves 34
  milling 21, 74, 75, 77
  names 18
  range 18, 21, 34, 73
  spacing 75
  uses 21
Bigleaf Maple Managers' Handbook 29
bleach 46, 70
boiling down 55, 88
bottling 62
Brix 88
bubbles 61
bud burst 69, 88
buddy 23, 27, 88

C
calcium 21, 70, 73
cambium layer 30, 88
canning 62
chlorine. *See* bleach
cleaning equipment 70
containers 45, 65
cooking 21
coppice 11, 37, 76, 88
crop rotation 77
crown 38, 88

D
decay 74
dormant season 89
drill bit 39
drilling 39
dropline 43, 89

E
east and west sugaring differences 20
egg clarification 58, 88
equipment
  cleaning 70
  food-rated 44, 89
  list of recommended 25
  pan 55, 89
  suppliers 86
evaporation 51
evaporator 89
evaporator types
  commercial 53
  homemade 53
  hot plate 52
  kitchen stove 52
  propane burner 52
  woodstove 52

F
fermenting 43
filtering 49, 58, 89
finishing 57
flavour. *See* syrup: flavour
Flavour Wheel 66, 89
foam 56
food-rated 44, 89
food safety 51

G
girdling 89

H
habitat 73
heartwood 89
hydrometer 33, 59, 89

L
lumber. *See* milling

M
managed forest 89
maple water 21, 89
milling 21, 74, 75, 77, 78
   checking 88
moisture 51
mould 59, 70

N
nitre. *See* sugar sand
non-timber 89
nutrients 21

O
Orlon 50, 58

P
pan 55, 89
phloem 90
photosynthesis 30, 90
plastic syrup jugs 63

R
recipes 81
refractometer 26, 33, 59, 89
respiration 90
Rule of 86 51, 90

S
sap
   bacteria 47
   collection 47
   collection system 43
   containers 45, 47
   cooking with 21, 81
   definition of 90
   fermenting 43
   flow 27
   storage 47
   sugar content 35
   yeast 47
sapwood 30, 90
scale of operation 24
site 38
spacing the stand 75
specific gravity 60
spiles 42, 90
   pulling 69
stem 90
storage 62
sugar content 59
sugar crystals 59
sugar sand 49, 58, 90
sugar shack 56, 90
sugarbush 90
sugaring 18, 89
syrup
   advertising 65
   apron 61
   bottling 62
   bubbles 61
   containers 62, 65
   definition of 90
   egg clarification 58, 88
   finishing 57
   flavour
      23, 27, 46, 55, 66, 70, 88
   Flavour Wheel 66, 89
   grading rules 63

syrup *(continued)*
  labeling 63
  making 51–66
  mould 59
  quality. *See* syrup: flavour
  recipes 83
  sap level 55
  skimming foam 56, 59
  specific gravity 60
  storage 62
  sugar crystals 59
  sugar sand 49, 90
  temperature test 60

T

tap 91
tap holes
  drilling 39
  healing over 41
  height 40
tapping
  choosing the trees 35
  drilling 39
tapping season 23, 69, 91
tees 45, 91
temperature test for sugar
    content 60
transpiration 91
tree
  age 36
  crown 38, 88
  exposure 38
  form 37
  health 74
  site 38
  size 38
  stand management 73
  wounds 37
trunk size 38
tubing 43, 91

V

vegetable oil jugs 46

W

wet sites 38
wine 22, 47
wolf tree 38, 91
woodlot 91
wounds 37

Y

yeast 47, 70

To order more copies or enquire about the book

Bigleaf Sugaring
Tapping the western maple

Please write, email or call

Backwoods Forest Management
12691 South Doole Road
Ladysmith, British Columbia
V9G 1J6   Canada

Phone: 250-245-4939
Email: blmaple@telus.net
www.blmaple.net

Please send _____ copy(ies) of **Bigleaf Sugaring** (ISBN 0-9736206-0-9) at $15.00 (includes taxes) plus $4.00 shipping and handling to:

Name: _____

Mailing Address: _____

City, Province: _____

Postal Code: _____

Phone or email address: _____

Make cheques payable to **Teesh Backlund**
All orders must be prepaid

About Backlund's Backwoods and the authors

Backlund's Backwoods is a small-scale, family run managed forest (BC #127) overlooking Ladysmith Harbour on Vancouver Island. It is owned and operated by Gary & Teesh Backlund, and their daughter and son-in-law, Katherine & Devan Banman.

The Backlund's are founding members of the Private Forest Landowners Association and the South Island Woodlot Association. Katherine has her Forest Resources Technology Diploma and a certificate in Horticulture, both from Vancouver Island University (VIU). Gary currently works part-time teaching carpentry at VIU and Teesh is now retired. Gary and Katherine are volunteer wardens for the Woodley Range Ecological Reserve.

Although growing and selling logs was their original goal, they quickly realized that "value-added" and non-timber products are critical to making a living from only 70 acres of forestland. Value-added products include air-dried lumber for hobby and commercial woodworkers. Non-timber products include arbutus branches for bird toys and perches, arbutus stumps for turning and carving, sequoia greens for the floral market and, of course, maple syrup.

Keeping the environment and aesthetics in mind, they strive to maintain a park-like setting while practicing forestry. The Backlund's comment that many of their practices reflect their forest's small size and would not be economically practical in a larger-scale forestry operation. As the Backlunds reside on their forest property, much of the management work has become family recreation, working together in their backwoods.

Philosophy

Gary states, "We like to be creative in our approach to forestry. Life and all we do should be a learning experience".

Teesh adds, "We are thankful for being blessed with the opportunity of living and working in such beautiful surroundings and hope the management of our woodland and our stewardship practices will make a positive contribution to the Ladysmith community."

Katherine says, "Nature and the forest provide entertainment, recreation and a peaceful environment, a great place to live."

Gary, Teesh and Katherine can be reached by email at blmaple@telus.net
You can visit their website at http://www.blmaple.net